Birding
in Baja California Sur

American Kestrel

Snowy Egret

Table of Contents

Shorelines & Dunes

Brown Pelicans and Herring Gulls

Franklin's Gull

Royal Tern

Bonaparte's Gulls

Least Tern

Snowy Plover

Brown Pelicans Feeding with Dolphins

Osprey Fishing

Caspian Terns

Estuaries

Magnificent Frigatebird

Black-crowned Night-Heron Juv

Long-billed Dowitcher

Greater White-fronted Goose

Tricolored Heron

Great Egret

Northern Pintail

Clark's Grebe

American Coots

Snowy Egrets

Brown Pelican

Common Gallinule

Bufflehead

Little Blue Heron

Eared Grebe

White-faced Ibis

Belding's Yellowthroat and Black Phoebe

Spotted Sandpiper

Black-necked Stilts

Palm Oases

Gila Woodpecker M

Hooded Oriole F

Hooded Oriole M

Hooded Oriole Juv

Scott's Oriole M

Wilson's Warbler M

Yellow Warbler F

Western Tanager

Great Horned Owl

Wilson's Warbler F

Green-tailed Towhee

Western Scrub Jay

California Quail

Little Green Heron

Xantus's Hummingbird F

Belding's Yellowthroat

Black-headed Grosbeak

Yellow-headed Blackbird F

Common Ground-Dove Nest

Common Ground-Dove Juv

White-winged Doves

Northern Mockingbird Juv

White-winged Doves

Cactus Wren Nest

Great Egret

Gray Thrasher

Crested Caracara Juv

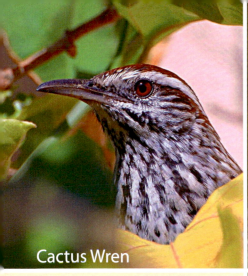

Cactus Wren

Costa's Hummingbirds

Gila Woodpecker M

Red-tailed Hawk

Gilded Flicker Dispute

Scott's Oriole, Hooded Oriole
and Cactus Wren

California Quail

Harris's Hawks

Verdin

Vesper Sparrows

Rock Dove

Purple Martin

Northern Rough-winged Swallows

Common Ground-Dove

Costa's Hummingbird

Cactus Wrens

Cassin's Kingbird

Hooded Oriole F, Gila Woodpecker and White-winged Dove

American Kestrel with House Finches

Phainopepla M

Blue Grosbeak

Northern Mockingbird

Northern Cardinal M

Islands, Bays & Mangroves

White Ibis

American Oystercatcher

Double-crested Cormorant   Yellow-footed Gull

Reddish Egret

Double-crested Cormorant Juv

Brandt's Cormorants

Marbled Godwits

Blue-footed Boobies

Great Blue Heron

Whimbrel and Red Knot

Great Blue Heron

Yellow-footed Gulls

Sierra de la Laguna

Greater Roadrunner

Brown-headed Cowbird

Lesser Goldfinches F

Lazuli Bunting

Bell's Vireo

Common Raven

Eurasian Collared-Doves

Ladder-backed Woodpecker

Northern Cardinal F

Blue Grosbeaks

Black Phoebe

Anna's Hummingbird M

Rufous Hummingbird M

Lark Sparrows

Orange-crowned Warblers

Cooper's Hawk Juv

Cassin's Kingbirds, House Finches and Lesser Goldfinches

Raptors

American Kestrel

Zone-tailed Hawk

Harris's Hawk

Red-tailed Hawk (Dark Phase)

American Kestrel

Peregrine Falcon

Crested Caracara

Crested Caracaras

Osprey

Recyclers

Turkey Vultures

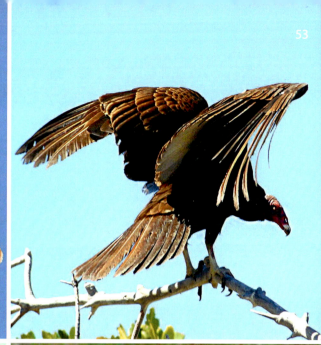

Turkey Vultures

Brandt's Cormorant

White-winged Dove

ANSERIFORMES: Anatidae

Fulvous Whistling-Duck .... *Dendrocygna bicolor*
Greater White-fronted Goose .... *Anser albifrons*
Brant .... *Branta bernicla*
Cackling Goose .... *Branta hutchinsii*
Canada Goose .... *Branta canadensis*
Gadwall .... *Anas strepera*
American Wigeon .... *Anas americana*
Mallard .... *Anas platyrhynchos*
Blue-winged Teal .... *Anas discors*
Cinnamon Teal .... *Anas cyanoptera*
Northern Shoveler .... *Anas clypeata*
Northern Pintail .... *Anas acuta*
Green-winged Teal .... *Anas crecca*
Canvasback .... *Aythya valisineria*
Redhead .... *Aythya americana*
Ring-necked Duck .... *Aythya collaris*
Lesser Scaup .... *Aythya affinis*
Surf Scoter .... *Melanitta perspicillata*
Bufflehead .... *Bucephala albeola*
Common Goldeneye .... *Bucephala clangula*
Red-breasted Merganser .... *Mergus serrator*
Ruddy Duck .... *Oxyura jamaicensis*

GALLIFORMES: Odontophoridae

California Quail .... *Callipepla californica*

GAVIIFORMES: Gaviidae

Red-throated Loon .... *Gavia stellata*
Pacific Loon .... *Gavia pacifica*
Common Loon .... *Gavia immer*

PODICIPEDIFORMES: Podicipedidae

Least Grebe .... *Tachybaptus dominicus*
Pied-billed Grebe .... *Podilymbus podiceps*
Horned Grebe .... *Podiceps auritus*
Eared Grebe .... *Podiceps nigricollis*
Western Grebe .... *Aechmophorus occidentalis*
Clark's Grebe .... *Aechmophorus clarkii*

PROCELLARIIFORMES: Diomedeidae

Laysan Albatross .... *Phoebastria immutabilis*
Black-footed Albatross .... *Phoebastria nigripes*

PROCELLARIIFORMES: Procellariidae

Northern Fulmar .... *Fulmarus glacialis*
Kermadec Petrel .... *Pterodroma neglecta*
Juan Fernandez Petrel .... *Pterodroma externa*
Galapagos Petrel .... *Pterodroma phaeopygia*
Cook's Petrel .... *Pterodroma cookii*

Pink-footed Shearwater .... *Puffinus creatopus*
Wedge-tailed Shearwater .... *Puffinus pacificus*
Sooty Shearwater .... *Puffinus griseus*
Galapagos Shearwater .... *Puffinus subalaris*
Townsend's Shearwater .... *Puffinus auricularis*
Black-vented Shearwater .... *Puffinus opisthomelas*

PROCELLARIIFORMES: Hydrobatidae

Leach's Storm-Petrel .... *Oceanodroma leucorhoa*
Ashy Storm-Petrel .... *Oceanodroma homochroa*
Wedge-rumped Storm-Petrel .... *Oceanodroma tethys*
Black Storm-Petrel .... *Oceanodroma melania*
Guadalupe Storm-Petrel .... *Oceanodroma macrodactyla*
Least Storm-Petrel .... *Oceanodroma microsoma*

PHAETHONTIFORMES: Phaethontidae

Red-billed Tropicbird .... *Phaethon aethereus*
Red-tailed Tropicbird .... *Phaethon rubricauda*

SULIFORMES: Fregatidae

Magnificent Frigatebird .... *Fregata magnificens*
Great Frigatebird .... *Fregata minor*

SULIFORMES: Sulidae

Masked Booby .... *Sula dactylatra*
Nazca Booby .... *Sula granti*
Blue-footed Booby .... *Sula nebouxii*
Brown Booby .... *Sula leucogaster*
Red-footed Booby .... *Sula sula*

SULIFORMES: Phalacrocoracidae

Brandt's Cormorant .... *Phalacrocorax penicillatus*
Neotropic Cormorant .... *Phalacrocorax brasilianus*
Double-crested Cormorant .... *Phalacrocorax auritus*
Pelagic Cormorant .... *Phalacrocorax pelagicus*

PELECANIFORMES: Pelecanidae

American White Pelican .... *Pelecanus erythrorhynchos*
Brown Pelican .... *Pelecanus occidentalis*

PELECANIFORMES: Ardeidae

American Bittern .... *Botaurus lentiginosus*
Least Bittern .... *Ixobrychus exilis*
Great Blue Heron .... *Ardea herodias*
Great Egret .... *Ardea alba*
Snowy Egret .... *Egretta thula*
Little Blue Heron .... *Egretta caerulea*
Tricolored Heron .... *Egretta tricolor*
Reddish Egret .... *Egretta rufescens*
Cattle Egret .... *Bubulcus ibis*

PELECANIFORMES: Ardeidae

Green Heron .... *Butorides virescens*

PELECANIFORMES: Ardeidae cont.

Black-crowned Night-Heron.......... *Nycticorax nycticorax*
Yellow-crowned Night-Heron .... *Nyctanassa violacea*

PELECANIFORMES: Threskiornithidae

White Ibis.................................. *Eudocimus albus*
White-faced Ibis.......................... *Plegadis chihi*
Roseate Spoonbill .... *Platalea ajaja*

ACCIPITRIFORMES: Cathartidae

Turkey Vulture .... *Cathartes aura*

ACCIPITRIFORMES: Pandioninae

Osprey...................................... *Pandion haliaetus*

ACCIPITRIFORMES: Accipitridae

Mississippi Kite........................... *Ictinia mississippiensis*
Northern Harrier .... *Circus cyaneus*
Sharp-shinned Hawk .... *Accipiter striatus*
Cooper's Hawk............................ *Accipiter cooperii*
Common Black-Hawk.................... *Buteogallus anthracinus*
Harris's Hawk.............................. *Parabuteo unicinctus*
Red-shouldered Hawk................... *Buteo lineatus*
Gray Hawk................................. *Buteo plagiatus*
Short-tailed Hawk....................... *Buteo brachyurus*
Zone-tailed Hawk........................ *Buteo albonotatus*
Red-tailed Hawk .... *Buteo jamaicensis*
Ferruginous Hawk .... *Buteo regalis*
Golden Eagle.............................. *Aquila chrysaetos*

GRUIFORMES: Rallidae

Black Rail .... *Laterallus jamaicensis*
Clapper Rail............................... *Rallus longirostris*
Virginia Rail............................... *Rallus limicola*
Sora.. *Porzana carolina*
Purple Gallinule .... *Porphyrio martinicus*
Common Gallinule .... *Gallinula galeata*
American Coot............................ *Fulica americana*

CHARADRIIFORMES: Recurvirostridae

Black-necked Stilt .... *Himantopus mexicanus*
American Avocet.......................... *Recurvirostra americana*

CHARADRIIFORMES: Haematopodidae

American Oystercatcher .... *Haematopus palliatus*
Black Oystercatcher...................... *Haematopus bachmani*

CHARADRIIFORMES: Charadriidae

Black-bellied Plover .... *Pluvialis squatarola*
Pacific Golden-Plover .... *Pluvialis fulva*
Snowy Plover .... *Charadrius nivosus*
Wilson's Plover .... *Charadrius wilsonia*
Semipalmated Plover.................... *Charadrius semipalmatus*
Killdeer .... *Charadrius vociferus*

CHARADRIIFORMES: Scolopacidae

Spotted Sandpiper .... *Actitis macularius*
Solitary Sandpiper .... *Tringa solitaria*
Wandering Tattler .... *Tringa incana*
Greater Yellowlegs....................... *Tringa melanoleuca*
Willet .... *Tringa semipalmata*
Lesser Yellowlegs .... *Tringa flavipes*
Whimbrel................................... *Numenius phaeopus*
Long-billed Curlew...................... *Numenius americanus*
Marbled Godwit .... *Limosa fedoa*
Ruddy Turnstone .... *Arenaria interpres*
Black Turnstone .... *Arenaria melanocephala*
Red Knot .... *Calidris canutus*
Surfbird.................................... *Calidris virgata*
Sanderling .... *Calidris alba*
Dunlin .... *Calidris alpina*
Baird's Sandpiper .... *Calidris bairdii*
Least Sandpiper .... *Calidris minutilla*
Buff-breasted Sandpiper .... *Calidris subruficollis*
Pectoral Sandpiper .... *Calidris melanotos*
Semipalmated Sandpiper.............. *Calidris pusilla*
Western Sandpiper....................... *Calidris mauri*
Short-billed Dowitcher.................. *Limnodromus griseus*
Long-billed Dowitcher .... *Limnodromus scolopaceus*
Wilson's Snipe .... *Gallinago delicata*
Wilson's Phalarope .... *Phalaropus tricolor*
Red-necked Phalarope .... *Phalaropus lobatus*
Red Phalarope............................ *Phalaropus fulicarius*

CHARADRIIFORMES: Stercorariidae

South Polar Skua .... *Stercorarius maccormicki*
Pomarine Jaeger .... *Stercorarius pomarinus*
Parasitic Jaeger .... *Stercorarius parasiticus*
Long-tailed Jaeger .... *Stercorarius longicaudus*

CHARADRIIFORMES: Alcidae

Guadalupe Murrelet .... *Synthliboramphus hypoleucus*
Craveri's Murrelet .... *Synthliboramphus craveri*
Ancient Murrelet .... *Synthliboramphus antiquus*
Cassin's Auklet........................... *Ptychoramphus aleuticus*
Rhinoceros Auklet .... *Cerorhinca monocerata*

CHARADRIIFORMES: Laridae

Black-legged Kittiwake .... *Rissa tridactyla*
Sabine's Gull.............................. *Xema sabini*
Bonaparte's Gull .... *Chroicocephalus philadelphia*
Laughing Gull............................. *Leucophaeus atricilla*
Heermann's Gull .... *Larus heermanni*
Mew Gull................................... *Larus canus*

CHARADRIIFORMES: Laridae cont.

Franklin's Gull .... *Larus pipixcan*
Ring-billed Gull .... *Larus delawarensis*
Western Gull .... *Larus occidentalis*
Yellow-footed Gull .... *Larus livens*
California Gull .... *Larus californicus*
Herring Gull..................................... *Larus argentatus*
Thayer's Gull .... *Larus thayeri*
Glaucous-winged Gull .... *Larus glaucescens*
Brown Noddy .... *Anous stolidus*
Sooty Tern .... *Onychoprion fuscatus*
Least Tern...................................... *Sternula antillarum*
Gull-billed Tern.............................. *Gelochelidon nilotica*
Caspian Tern .... *Hydroprogne caspia*
Black Tern...................................... *Chlidonias niger*
Common Tern .... *Sterna hirundo*
Arctic Tern .... *Sterna paradisaea*
Forster's Tern .... *Sterna forsteri*
Royal Tern...................................... *Thalasseus maximus*
Elegant Tern .... *Thalasseus elegans*
Black Skimmer .... *Rynchops niger*

COLUMBIFORMES: Columbidae

Rock Pigeon .... *Columba livia*
Eurasian Collared-Dove .... *Streptopelia decaocto*
White-winged Dove .... *Zenaida asiatica*
Mourning Dove .... *Zenaida macroura*
Socorro Dove .... *Zenaida graysoni*
Inca Dove .... *Columbina inca*
Common Ground-Dove.................. *Columbina passerina*

CUCULIFORMES: Cuculidae

Yellow-billed Cuckoo .... *Coccyzus americanus*
Greater Roadrunner .... *Geococcyx californianus*

STRIGIFORMES: Tytonidae

Barn Owl .... *Tyto alba*

STRIGIFORMES: Strigidae

Western Screech-Owl .... *Megascops kennicottii*
Great Horned Owl.......................... *Bubo virginianus*
Northern Pygmy-Owl .... *Glaucidium gnoma*
Elf Owl... *Micrathene whitneyi*
Burrowing Owl .... *Athene cunicularia*
Short-eared Owl .... *Asio flammeus*

CAPRIMULGIFORMES: Caprimulgidae

Lesser Nighthawk........................... *Chordeiles acutipennis*
Common Pauraque......................... *Nyctidromus albicollis*
Common Poorwill .... *Phalaenoptilus nuttallii*
Mexican Whip-poor-will .... *Antrostomus arizonae*

APODIFORMES: Apodidae

Black Swift .... *Cypseloides niger*
Vaux's Swift.................................... *Chaetura vauxi*
White-throated Swift .... *Aeronautes saxatalis*

APODIFORMES: Trochilidae

Black-chinned Hummingbird .... *Archilochus alexandri*
Anna's Hummingbird .... *Calypte anna*
Costa's Hummingbird .... *Calypte costae*
Rufous Hummingbird...................... *Selasphorus rufus*
Xantus's Hummingbird.................... *Hylocharis xantusii*

CORACIIFORMES: Alcedinidae

Belted Kingfisher .... *Megaceryle alcyon*
Green Kingfisher .... *Chloroceryle americana*

PICIFORMES: Picidae

Lewis's Woodpecker .... *Melanerpes lewis*
Gila Woodpecker .... *Melanerpes uropygialis*
Williamson's Sapsucker .... *Sphyrapicus thyroideus*
Yellow-bellied Sapsucker .... *Sphyrapicus varius*
Red-naped Sapsucker .... *Sphyrapicus nuchalis*
Red-breasted Sapsucker................ *Sphyrapicus ruber*
Ladder-backed Woodpecker.......... *Picoides scalaris*
Northern Flicker .... *Colaptes auratus*
Gilded Flicker .... *Colaptes chrysoides*
Pale-billed Woodpecker .... *Campephilus guatemalensis*

FALCONIFORMES: Falconidae

Crested Caracara............................ *Caracara cheriway*
American Kestrel .... *Falco sparverius*
Merlin .... *Falco columbarius*
Peregrine Falcon............................ *Falco peregrinus*
Prairie Falcon................................. *Falco mexicanus*

PSITTACIFORMES: Psittacidae

Green Parakeet............................... *Aratinga holochlora*

PASSERIFORMES: Tyrannidae

Western Wood-Pewee..................... *Contopus sordidulus*
Alder Flycatcher .... *Empidonax alnorum*
Willow Flycatcher........................... *Empidonax traillii*
Least Flycatcher............................. *Empidonax minimus*
Hammond's Flycatcher .... *Empidonax hammondii*
Gray Flycatcher............................. *Empidonax wrightii*
Dusky Flycatcher .... *Empidonax oberholseri*
Pacific-slope Flycatcher .... *Empidonax difficilis*
Black Phoebe .... *Sayornis nigricans*
Say's Phoebe .... *Sayornis saya*
Vermilion Flycatcher...................... *Pyrocephalus rubinus*
Ash-throated Flycatcher .... *Myiarchus cinerascens*
Great Crested Flycatcher .... *Myiarchus crinitus*

PASSERIFORMES: Tyrannidae cont.

Sulphur-bellied Flycatcher .... *Myiodynastes luteiventris*

Cassin's Kingbird............................ *Tyrannus vociferans*

PASSERIFORMES: Laniidae

Loggerhead Shrike .... *Lanius ludovicianus*

PASSERIFORMES: Vireonidae

White-eyed Vireo .... *Vireo griseus*

Bell's Vireo.................................... *Vireo bellii*

Gray Vireo..................................... *Vireo vicinior*

Plumbeous Vireo .... *Vireo plumbeus*

Cassin's Vireo .... *Vireo cassinii*

Blue-headed Vireo .... *Vireo solitarius*

Warbling Vireo .... *Vireo gilvus*

Philadelphia Vireo .... *Vireo philadelphicus*

Red-eyed Vireo.............................. *Vireo olivaceus*

Yellow-green Vireo .... *Vireo flavoviridis*

PASSERIFORMES: Corvidae

Black-throated Magpie-Jay .... *Calocitta colliei*

Western Scrub-Jay .... *Aphelocoma californica*

Chihuahuan Raven .... *Corvus cryptoleucus*

Common Raven.............................. *Corvus corax*

PASSERIFORMES: Alaudidae

Horned Lark .... *Eremophila alpestris*

PASSERIFORMES: Hirundinidae

Purple Martin................................ *Progne subis*

Tree Swallow................................. *Tachycineta bicolor*

Violet-green Swallow.................... *Tachycineta thalassina*

Northern Rough-winged Swallow   *Stelgidopteryx serripennis*

Bank Swallow .... *Riparia riparia*

Cliff Swallow .... *Petrochelidon pyrrhonota*

Barn Swallow .... *Hirundo rustica*

PASSERIFORMES: Paridae

Juniper Titmouse.......................... *Baeolophus ridgwayi*

PASSERIFORMES: Remizidae

Verdin .... *Auriparus flaviceps*

PASSERIFORMES: Aegithalidae

Bushtit .... *Psaltriparus minimus*

PASSERIFORMES: Sittidae

Red-breasted Nuthatch................. *Sitta canadensis*

PASSERIFORMES: Troglodytidae

Rock Wren..................................... *Salpinctes obsoletus*

Canyon Wren .... *Catherpes mexicanus*

House Wren................................... *Troglodytes aedon*

Socorro Wren................................. *Troglodytes sissonii*

Clarion Wren .... *Troglodytes tanneri*

Marsh Wren................................... *Cistothorus palustris*

Bewick's Wren .... *Thryomanes bewickii*

Cactus Wren .... *Campylorhynchus brunneicapillus*

PASSERIFORMES: Polioptilidae

Blue-gray Gnatcatcher .... *Polioptila caerulea*

California Gnatcatcher.................... *Polioptila californica*

Black-tailed Gnatcatcher .... *Polioptila melanura*

PASSERIFORMES: Regulidae

Ruby-crowned Kinglet .... *Regulus calendula*

PASSERIFORMES: Turdidae

Mountain Bluebird .... *Sialia currucoides*

Townsend's Solitaire...................... *Myadestes townsendi*

Swainson's Thrush .... *Catharus ustulatus*

Hermit Thrush .... *Catharus guttatus*

Varied Thrush .... *Ixoreus naevius*

PASSERIFORMES: Mimidae

Gray Catbird .... *Dumetella carolinensis*

Gray Thrasher .... *Toxostoma cinereum*

Le Conte's Thrasher .... *Toxostoma lecontei*

Sage Thrasher................................ *Oreoscoptes montanus*

Socorro Mockingbird .... *Mimus graysoni*

Northern Mockingbird.................... *Mimus polyglottos*

PASSERIFORMES: Sturnidae

European Starling .... *Sturnus vulgaris*

PASSERIFORMES: Motacillidae

American Pipit .... *Anthus rubescens*

Sprague's Pipit .... *Anthus spragueii*

PASSERIFORMES: Bombycillidae

Cedar Waxwing .... *Bombycilla cedrorum*

PASSERIFORMES: Ptiliogonatidae

Phainopepla.................................. *Phainopepla nitens*

PASSERIFORMES: Parulidae

Ovenbird .... *Seiurus aurocapilla*

Northern Waterthrush.................... *Parkesia noveboracensis*

Golden-winged Warbler.................. *Vermivora chrysoptera*

Black-and-white Warbler .... *Mniotilta varia*

Prothonotary Warbler .... *Protonotaria citrea*

Orange-crowned Warbler.............. *Oreothlypis celata*

Virginia's Warbler .... *Oreothlypis virginiae*

MacGillivray's Warbler .... *Geothlypis tolmiei*

Kentucky Warbler .... *Geothlypis formosa*

Belding's Yellowthroat .... *Geothlypis beldingi*

Common Yellowthroat.................... *Geothlypis trichas*

Hooded Warbler .... *Setophaga citrina*

American Redstart .... *Setophaga ruticilla*

PASSERIFORMES: Parulidae cont.

Cape May Warbler .... *Setophaga tigrina*
Cerulean Warbler............................ *Setophaga cerulea*
Northern Parula .... *Setophaga americana*
Blackburnian Warbler..................... *Setophaga fusca*
Yellow Warbler .... *Setophaga petechia*
Yellow-rumped Warbler .... *Setophaga coronata*
Prairie Warbler .... *Setophaga discolor*
Grace's Warbler.............................. *Setophaga graciae*
Black-throated Gray Warbler .... *Setophaga nigrescens*
Townsend's Warbler .... *Setophaga townsendi*
Black-throated Green Warbler .... *Setophaga virens*
Canada Warbler............................. *Cardellina canadensis*
Wilson's Warbler............................ *Cardellina pusilla*
Yellow-breasted Chat .... *Icteria virens*

PASSERIFORMES: Emberizidae

White-collared Seedeater .... *Sporophila torqueola*
Green-tailed Towhee .... *Pipilo chlorurus*
California Towhee........................... *Melozone crissalis*
Botteri's Sparrow........................... *Peucaea botterii*
Cassin's Sparrow .... *Peucaea cassinii*
Chipping Sparrow .... *Spizella passerina*
Clay-colored Sparrow .... *Spizella pallida*
Brewer's Sparrow .... *Spizella breweri*
Black-chinned Sparrow .... *Spizella atrogularis*
Vesper Sparrow .... *Pooecetes gramineus*
Lark Sparrow................................. *Chondestes grammacus*
Black-throated Sparrow .... *Amphispiza bilineata*
Lark Bunting .... *Calamospiza melanocorys*
Savannah Sparrow .... *Passerculus sandwichensis*
Grasshopper Sparrow.................... *Ammodramus savannarum*
Song Sparrow................................ *Melospiza melodia*
Lincoln's Sparrow .... *Melospiza lincolnii*
Swamp Sparrow............................. *Melospiza georgiana*
White-crowned Sparrow............... *Zonotrichia leucophrys*
Yellow-eyed Junco .... *Junco phaeonotus*

PASSERIFORMES: Cardinalidae

Western Tanager .... *Piranga ludoviciana*
Northern Cardinal .... *Cardinalis cardinalis*
Pyrrhuloxia.................................... *Cardinalis sinuatus*

PASSERIFORMES: Icteridae (cont.)

Black-headed Grosbeak................. *Pheucticus melanocephalus*
Blue Grosbeak .... *Passerina caerulea*
Lazuli Bunting............................... *Passerina amoena*
Varied Bunting .... *Passerina versicolor*

PASSERIFORMES: Icteridae

Yellow-headed Blackbird .... *Xanthocephalus xanthocephalus*
Red-winged Blackbird................... *Agelaius phoeniceus*
Eastern Meadowlark .... *Sturnella magna*
Western Meadowlark .... *Sturnella neglecta*
Brewer's Blackbird......................... *Euphagus cyanocephalus*
Great-tailed Grackle .... *Quiscalus mexicanus*
Bronzed Cowbird........................... *Molothrus aeneus*
Brown-headed Cowbird .... *Molothrus ater*
Hooded Oriole .... *Icterus cucullatus*
Streak-backed Oriole .... *Icterus pustulatus*
Bullock's Oriole............................. *Icterus bullockii*
Baltimore Oriole............................ *Icterus galbula*
Scott's Oriole .... *Icterus parisorum*

PASSERIFORMES: Fringillidae

House Finch.................................... *Haemorhous mexicanus*
Cassin's Finch................................ *Haemorhous cassinii*
Lesser Goldfinch .... *Spinus psaltria*
American Goldfinch........................ *Spinus tristis*

PASSERIFORMES: Passeridae

House Sparrow............................... *Passer domesticus*

Avibase Bird Checklists of the World Baja California Sur courtesy of Denis Lepage. Lepage, D. 2013. Checklist of the birds of Baja California Sur, Mexico. Avibase, the World Database. http://avibase.bsc-eoc.org/checklist.jsp?region=MXbs

Killdeer

Xantus's Hummingbirds

Index of Bird Photos

Reddish Egret

Great Egrets

We would like to acknowledge the following individuals for sharing their tremendous knowledge, strength and creativity in bringing this project to fruition:

Thea Thomas
Janice Kinne
Patrick Nicholas
Kate Turning
Denis Lepage
Fabrice Serriere
Umberto (Beto) Domínguez
La Gisela
Milagros
Chapo
La Princessa